# Golf 97

GW01390797

## Surprisingly Simple Secrets

### How you can turn frustration into pleasure!

# Introduction

Dear Fellow Golfing Enthusiast,

Hello and welcome to this series of tried and tested and proven tips that are certain to help you in every area of your game. To make it easy for you to use these tips they've been laid out in the most obvious way. Starting with the mental side of the game and proceeding through course management, driving, iron play, chipping and putting. At the end of the book you'll find some useful thoughts about equipment, rules & etiquette and scoring.

Dip into the book to find a specific tip on an area of your game where you need some advice - or read through all of the tips in one quick session. Then review the tips from time to time until you know all the ideas and can apply them whenever you need them. You know that by practice and as you easily apply these ideas you'll soon be one of the fortunate few who enjoy every moment of their golfing game. You'll be one of those who win more often, get the applause and definitely take home the prizes.

Golf is a game, a game to be enjoyed. It's the ideal way to make new friends, get involved in social activities and travel to some of the most beautiful places on the planet. Use every golfing occasion to improve your game, to enjoy the scenery and to reach the goals you've set for yourself. With the advent of superior clubs and balls even advancing age won't stop you being able to still drive it far down the fairway, get backspin on the greens and shoot a score of which you're justly proud.

Enjoy the journey!

Danny Peck and Peter Thomson

# Mental **Preparation**

As with all sport a major part of your success at golf will be determined by your mental preparation, your mental state and your mental resilience when things don't go exactly as you'd like. The greatest achievers in any human endeavour, including the fascinating game of golf, realise that to play at their best they must be in total control of their mental faculties and thought processes. These are the deciding factors in your success. Take a moment now and read through the following tips. They will stand you in good stead for any game and help you fight off any negative thoughts.

**1** Set your goals every time you play - the easiest way to set goals at golf is to decide on 3 different targets. The gold goal - this is the score you really want, a goal that will stretch you to the utmost of your ability. The silver goal - this is a goal that will stretch you and is just out of reach, though not out of sight. The bronze goal - this is the worst case scenario that you'll accept. For example: a golfer playing off a handicap of 18 on a par 72 course might set a gold goal of 85 (5 shots under handicap) a silver goal of 88 (2 shots under handicap) and a bronze goal of 90 (on handicap) Always decide on your goals before you play - as the old expression says "If you don't know where you're going - all the roads lead there"

**2** Decide on your handicap reduction goal - A realistic handicap reduction goal is about 4 - 5 shots per year. Remember that the definition of a handicap is - an average score - not the occasional 67 or 68 that you may score.

**3** Visualise the shot before you play it - many of the greatest golfers throughout the ages have talked about seeing the shot in their mind's eye before they actually hit the ball. This is something you can do so easily. Just imagine if you could have a mulligan on every shot. Now you can! See the shot in your mind - that's the first one. Then play it for real - that's the second time you've played it. Don't be too surprised how much better you play when you always visualise a positive result.

**4** Maintain a positive attitude - always focus on the positive aspect of your game. Your mental attitude will determine how well you play. Listen to your opponents as they moan about the fact that they can't drive it straight, that they can't putt today or they're off their game. Those negative programmes aren't for you. Always use positive expressions about yourself and your game. There's always something to learn from every shot you take. Stay positive, stay focused and you'll stay on top. Remember your physical actions will always follow your mental state and programming. "What you say - will be the way"

**5** Be realistic in your expectations - if you haven't practised for a few days or didn't get chance to warm up your muscles before the game don't expect too much too soon. Always remember that unless you're a professional you play "The Game of Golf" not the "Business of Golf" It's a game you play for fun and the feeling of achievement. If you play off a handicap of 18 then every hole is a Par 5 for you. Use those shots wisely.

**6** Use anchoring techniques to build long-term muscle memory - Your mind has the marvellous ability to remember how to do things. When you create a link or anchor between great shots and another physical action (such as a clenched fist or pinch on the wrist) you can recreate the state you want by repeating that action. So, whenever you hit that drive 275 yards straight as an arrow - pinch your wrist. The next time you need that drive - pinch your wrist again and the muscle memory will be triggered. As a human being, part of your brain is called the Reptilian Brain - this enables you to repeat an action, once learned, over and over again - this is muscle memory in action. Many golfers have used this technique to slash shots off their handicap.

**7** Let go of bad shots - when you play a bad shot (doesn't everyone) rather than fretting about it or cursing and swearing simply say "5, 4, 3, 2, 1 - GONE! and let go of any negative feelings. You can't change the shot you've played so you might as well accept that it's happened and see how you can recover the situation. So many golfers carry the thought of a missed putt onto the next tee and see their drives end up in the rough or worse. Let go! "Accept what you can't change and change what you can't accept!" Remember - a bad shot is only a bad shot - if your next shot doesn't achieve the result you want. For example - you may top your drive just 50 yards and yet put your second shot three feet from the pin. The drive turned out to be - not that bad!

# **Course** Management

1 Play a shot you can play - Avoid playing that "one in a million shot" often called a - tin-cup shot or career shot. Make the shot you can make. I'm certain that you've seen fellow players "going for it" and ending up in trouble and suffering a 3 or 4 shot swing against them.

2 Play an iron off the tee. Sometimes it's better to lose a few yards in length rather than find water, bunkers or be stymied behind a tree. Many players disagree with this thought - however play your own game and give yourself every chance to take the fewest shots on every hole.

3 Take the penalty and smile - To score well it's essential to keep the ball in play. The best place is on the fairway. If you get into trouble take the penalty and get back on the fairway. Dropping one shot is better than dropping 2 or 3 shots.

4 Pick an intermediate target - a spot approximate 2 feet in front of the ball and in line with your intended landing point. Always take aim before taking a shot. Many successful ten-pin bowlers aim at the arrows on the lane rather than at the pins.

5 Have a game plan - just like a successful team, involved in any sport, it's essential to have a game plan before you hit the first ball from the first tee. Know your opponent's strengths and weaknesses. Stick to your game plan regardless what the other player might do.

Key thoughts:

# The Set Up

1   Hold the club in your fingers - unlike other bats or racquets the weight of the golf club is in the head of the club - therefore - the club should be held in the fingers and not in the palm of the hand. It will be difficult to keep the clubhead online if the grip is incorrect. As you look down at your grip you should see the top 2 knuckles of each hand.

2   Aim the clubface - set the leading edge of the club at a 90-degree angle to the target line. This is known as square or straight. The clubhead should not be laid flat to the floor as the shaft deflects through the shot. Allow the toe of the club to sit up slightly. Many clubs these days have the bottom two grooves painted. Keep these clean to make it easier to aim the clubface.

3   Position the ball in the right place - as the swing is not a perfect circle the ball should not be positioned in the middle of the stance. The best routine to use is this... start with your feet together and the ball on a line between them. Move your left foot 4-5 inches to the left (keep the foot straight) then, depending on which club you are using - move the right foot to the right. For example, with a seven iron move the right foot 8-9 inches to the right. Move the right foot wider for longer clubs and less for shorter clubs.

4   Never aim your body at the target - think of the line of your body and a line on which the ball will travel - as being a set of railway lines. As you can picture - your body is not aimed at the target but aimed at a point slightly to the left of the target. If you aim your body at the target you will have closed your shoulders slightly and the ball is likely to hook or draw. Left handed players would aim at a point slightly right of the target.

5   Create the right posture - to create the right posture stand bolt upright, with arms extended in front of you - with the club at waist level parallel to the floor. Then slightly tilt the clubhead so that it starts to point towards the ground. Then hinge forward from the waist, keeping your legs straight until the club touches the ground and then flex your knees. Your hands will now be directly below your chin and the butt end of the club approximately 4-5 inches from your legs. Maintain these angles with all clubs. Picture a goalkeeper in a soccer game ready to save a penalty shot - those body angles are ideal for playing great golf shots.

# Direction

1  Manoeuvre the ball around the course - most golfers would like to hit the ball in a straight line however this is not always possible. The clubface has grooves and the ball has dimples - both are designed to impart spin to the ball. Most golf courses contain very few holes that are dead straight so if you experience a hook or slice - play with it until you can learn to draw or fade - these shots give you more control over the ball. Use the spin to manoeuvre your way around the course in an effective manner.

2  Hook the ball around obstacles - a hook is when the ball travels sharply from right to left and can be used to get round obstacles such as trees or dog legs. The hook can produce additional distance because of the associated clubhead speed and de-lofting of the clubface. The ball flies lower which can be extremely useful in windy conditions. However there is less control as the ball will spin away from you once it has landed.

3  Use the slice to start the ball left and turn sharply right - many golfers are concerned about the slice however it can be used extremely effectively to get the ball over trees and out of bunkers. The slice has more height and more backspin on the ball. Be aware of the reduction in distance that the slice will achieve and select a longer club.

4  Use the draw to produce distance and control - the draw is really a controlled hook as the ball starts to the right and moves gently to the left during flight. To produce a draw it is necessary to look at the clubface and how it returns to the ball through the impact area. The forearms are the key to producing the draw. The forearms need to rotate anti-clockwise slightly to close the clubface at the point of impact and produce the draw. If this is overdone then the ball will hook. When attempting to draw the ball aim everything (club, ball and body) to the right of the target line to allow for the spin and the left to right flight.

5  Fade the ball to create more backspin - many of the world's top players use this type of shot when approaching the green because of the additional backspin created by the fade. During the fade the ball starts slightly left and moves gently to the right during flight. One of the best ways to hit a fade is to try and strike the ball with a square or straight clubface (returning the club back to the ball as it started). On most occasions the ball will spin with fade because most golfers hands are not fast enough to get the club face back to the ball in a straight position.

6  Use your hands and your head - the only part of the club in contact with the ball is the clubface and the only part of the club in contact with you is the grip - held in your hands. To produce all of the above shots you must tell the club what to do by rotating

it one way or another. Do not rely on good timing or the perfect swing. Simply programme your mind for the shot you wish to play and leave the rest to your body's natural ability to follow your mental programme.

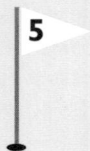

## 5 ▷ Long Irons

1. Consider the lie - when you approach a shot that requires a long iron the first question in your mind must be "how good is the lie of the ball?" It's inadvisable to attempt to play a long iron from heavy rough, small depressions or severe slopes. Use long irons from good lies.

2. Consider a 7 Wood - if you've found that your accuracy suffers when you use a long iron then consider using a utility club - such as a 7 wood or 9 wood. There are many different types to choose from. The beauty of these clubs is that they have mass and are heavy in the sole area allowing you to get the ball into the air with ease. You'll also find that shots from the rough are easier. The clubhead does not get tangled in the grass, unlike long irons.

3. Turn a full 90 degrees - some of the major problems that golfers experience with the use of long irons are no power or distance and the shot leaks to the right. Often this is caused by the lack of a full shoulder turn. The shoulders should turn 90 degrees both backwards and forwards. Avoid trying to steer the ball. Hitting long irons is like using a gun. Aim - set - pull the trigger!

4. Use an in-to-out swing path - the swing path is the line the club takes just before and just after impact with the ball. The most effective way to hit any object with power and direction is to attack the inside. Think of hitting a tennis ball. The racquet will be behind you at the start and once contact is made will swing away from you. When you practice with long irons align the maker's name on the ball - slightly to the right of your target line. Aim to swing the club on that line. This will promote an "in to out" swing.

5. Remain positive - avoid any negative thoughts when using long irons. Don't try to make your back swing slow and the down swing fast. This will cause a lack of awareness of the clubhead speed and your timing will suffer. Check the lie, choose the right club, maintain your rhythm, attack the inside and be positive! You'll find that your long irons are as easy to use as your short irons.

# Using **Woods**

**1** Set your tee height carefully - the height of the tee is dependent upon the player, the club, the design of the club and the conditions. You will know or have been told that the recommended tee height is half the ball above the face of the club. However, modern clubs that are made from titanium are much lighter than steel and so the manufacturer will have added weight to the club head. This weight usually lowers the centre of gravity of the club to enable the ball to get into the air more easily. Therefore it may be possible to tee the ball lower and still achieve the flight path you desire.

**2** Tee the ball higher in the wind - contrary to popular opinion it is necessary to tee the ball higher rather than lower when hitting into the wind. If the ball is teed lower it will force you to hit down on the ball. This will impart backspin and make the ball rise. This is what you're trying to avoid. Try different set-height tee pegs until you are comfortable in setting the ball at the right height.

**3** Take into account ... dynamic loft - Many golfers are able to hit their 3 wood or 5 wood further than their driver. This is based on dynamic loft. If the clubhead does not produce enough speed then the club will de-loft itself. A 10-degree driver at only 80-mph of clubhead speed returns to the ball with only six degrees of loft. The ball goes low and not very far. That's why - when a 15 degree 3 wood at slower speed de-lofts itself it becomes the same face angle as your driver. If you get better results with a three wood or five wood... use them!

**4** Try something else when it doesn't work! - if you find that your driver isn't working on a particular day... then leave it in the bag! Remember when you're playing you only have one chance off the tee. After three or four holes you'll know if your driver is working that day. If it is... use it. If it isn't... don't use it. Far better to sacrifice a few yards in distance and be on the fairway than end up in the rough or out of bounds.

**5** Use the technology - whatever your opinion about the use of technology in the game of golf and - that many traditionalists believe that the game is getting far too easy... technology is here to stay. Modern golf clubs can make a huge difference to your driving accuracy and the distance you produce. If your budget allows - consider using a modern large headed driver. This often increases confidence by creating the feeling that you cannot possible miss the ball.

**6** Make your woods your friends - Many golfers have a favourite club, perhaps a six iron or seven iron. This is probably one that they feel they can rely on - probably the one they practise with the most. Make the wood your friend, practise with it and over time your confidence and your results will improve. When first using woods your initial shots may not get you the results you want. Persevere and don't judge your woods by the first few shots you play with them.

# Chipping and Pitching

**1** Select the right club for the job - one of the reasons why some golfers chip badly is that they instinctively reach for their pitching wedge when faced with a chip onto the green. Consider using different clubs dependent upon what lies in front of you. If there are no obstacles then perhaps a straight faced club such as a 7 iron would be ideal. Many professional golfers use a three wood when chipping from dense rough at the edge of the green. If there are obstacles in your way such as a bunker or a stream then it will be necessary to use a lofted faced club.

**2** Consider distance and direction - always evaluate the target and realise that on all short shots there will be flight and roll. With a less lofted club the ball will be in the air for one-third of the time and roll the rest of the way. With a lofted club the ball will be in the air for half of the time. Always allow for the amount of roll you'll get with these types of shot.

**3** Have the correct stance and technique - imagine these types of shots as throwing a ball underarm. Keep your feet close together to eliminate body movement, arms extended and elbows close together. This will also stop wrist movement. Unfortunately wrist action is the killer of these types of shots. As it allows the clubhead to work faster than the hands and makes it difficult to control the speed and loft of the ball. To improve your chipping use the same distance and speed both in the back swing and through the ball.

**4** Consider angles and tempo - when pitching consider the amount of stop you require. The ball will act in the same way as a plane landing on a runway. A plane landing on its nose would pull up sharply. A plane landing on its back wheels would continue to roll forwards. The ball acts in the same way. Tempo needs to be constant. No acceleration or deceleration through the ball as this can cause low and heavy shots.

**5** Spend time around the green - 60% of the game of golf is played from 90 yards and under. Most golfers will admit that it is in this area that they suffer the most. The reduction of your handicap is reliant on this part of the game. Spend more time around the green developing shots and confidence. Be versatile, try different clubs, different flights of the ball and different strokes to improve your game. Don't practise shots during a match. Leave practice for the practice ground.

# Bunkers

1. Be aware of the rules - The bunker is a hazard and you must be careful entering and leaving. Do not ground your club. The club must not touch the sand until you make the swing for the ball. Be careful what you remove from the bunker. You cannot touch anything that is alive or was alive [worms, leaves or twigs] Stones are subject to local rules, check the back of the scorecard.

2. Think carefully about which club to use - you do not always have to use a sand wedge. Sometimes, when there is no face to the bunker you may be able to putt the ball. When rain has made the sand wet and compact - consider using a pitching wedge instead of a sand wedge. The pitching wedge with its sharper face will cut through the wet sand unlike the sand wedge which, with its larger sole, is likely to bounce causing a low trajectory shot - which may hit the face of the bunker or fly over the green.

3. Swing fully - changing the length of swing can produce problems as deceleration may occur - leaving the ball in the bunker. Swing fully as though you had a 7 iron in your hands. Practise taking different amounts of sand with the ball, from no sand at all - to a couple of inches. Note how far the ball travels and how quickly it stops.

4. Don't always go for the flag - sometimes it's worth considering aiming sideways out of the bunker. If you believe that you cannot get the ball onto the green then it's far better to sacrifice only one shot rather than standing there covered in sand with the ball still at your feet.

5. Don't be greedy in fairway bunkers - always use a club with sufficient loft to enable you to clear the face of the trap. Don't always think of distance. In fairway bunkers your primary aim must be to get the ball back in play. Grip the club tighter than normal as this will contract the muscles and reduce wrist movement. Remain quite still and slightly rigid when swinging as this will help you take the ball cleanly from the sand.

# Putting

1. Use your natural accuracy - every human being has natural accuracy. How else would you be able to cross a road safely. Trust your body to be able to perform. Once you know what your goal is - getting the ball into the hole - then it's easier to score that goal.

2. Use dead weight on short putts. Pick a piece of grass or mark inside the hole and stroke the ball towards it. Use dead weight so that the last two rolls of the ball takes it into the hole. Be specific! Don't aim at the hole - aim at an exact mark within the hole. For example - in the game of darts if you are aiming at the bulls eye - you don't look at the whole board. Be precise with your target and goals.

3. Look at the green as you walk towards it - one of the best ways to spot the borrow on a putt is to examine the landscape of both the green and the surrounding area. It's easy to see the lie of the land from a distance. The green invariably slopes towards water. Check for ponds, lakes or sea.

4. Forget the dustbin lid effect - many golfers have been told to imagine a circle around the hole that is the same size as a dustbin lid and to aim the ball at that. As you want to make the putt it's far better to aim to hole it, than miss by a few feet.

5. Create a routine - as with the long game it's essential to create a routine with putting. Start by looking behind the ball and pass your eyes over the whole green. Then look from behind the flagstick towards the ball as well as from the ball to the flagstick. This will give you two different perspectives. Pace out the distance from the ball to the hole and programme your mental computer with the information. As you watch all professional golfers you will notice that they each have a distinctive and different routine for putting. Find the routine that suits you.

6. Practise putting regularly - most golfers who take the time to practice spend much of their practice time at the driving range and little or no time on the practice green. Whilst an hour practising putting may become boring, as little as five minutes practice per day equates to 2 hours per month. This will pay you handsome dividends in lower scores.

# Awkward **Lies**

**1** Weigh up the shot before you play it - all of the following tips relate to awkward lies. The severity of the lie will determine which choices you make in club and direction. Think carefully before making the shot. In many situations it's better to play the safest and easiest shot and get the ball back into play.

**2** Hitting from an uphill lie - the key point to remember with this shot is that because the ball is on an uphill lie it will have instant loft. It is therefore necessary to take at least one club bigger to obtain the distance you require. The ball should be positioned in the middle of your stance to avoid topping it.

**3** Hitting from a downhill lie - this is one of the hardest shots in golf, particularly if you need to chip over an obstacle and then want the ball to stop quickly. The position of the ball is critical because the club is going to strike the ground much earlier than normal. Therefore position the ball back in your stance so that it is at the point of natural contact. Take a more lofted club than normal to help get the ball in the air.

**4** Hitting from above the feet - take a club with a shorter shaft because the ball is closer to you. Aim to the right of the target line dependent upon the amount of slope from which you're playing because this "above the feet lie" will tend to produce a spin on the ball from right to left. This happens because the swing becomes flatter and more around your body causing the ball to hook in flight.

**5** Hitting from below the feet - take a club with a longer shaft because the ball is further away from you. Aim to the left of the target line because from this "below the feet lie" the ball will tend to move left to right in flight. This happens because the swing becomes steeper and more upright, causing the ball to fade in flight.

**6** Keep your shoulders parallel to the ground - subject to the type of lie you are facing you must always ensure that your shoulders are parallel to the ground. To do so you need to bend your knees and distribute your weight differently to maintain the correct posture.

**1** Keep the lower half of your body still - shots from awkward lies should be played with the arms and shoulders only - with the lower half of the body remaining still. It may be necessary to take a less lofted club to gain the distance you require. Good balance is the key to making good shots from awkward lies.

# Conditions

**1** Avoid fighting the wind - playing in the wind can be one of the most difficult conditions you face. We judge the wind in "number of clubs". A two club wind means that you'll need to take a seven iron instead of a nine iron into the wind and a nine iron instead of a seven iron with the wind. Never fight the wind, as you will waste valuable energy. If the wind is blowing hard from the left - then aim to the left. Consider using a less lofted club to keep the ball low.

**2** Prepare for wet weather days - carry extra golfing gloves on wet days. Keep these in a waterproof bag or container. If you use an umbrella, keep a towel in the spokes to keep the towel dry so that you can dry your hands and grips. If you are uncomfortable playing in a waterproof jacket then use two lambswool jumpers. The top jumper will become soaked but the inner one will remain relatively dry. You may find it easier to swing wearing two jumpers rather than a waterproof jacket. As with all things in golf... it's your choice.

**3** Use yellow balls into the sun - playing into the low winter sun can make it difficult to see the ball. Ask your playing partners to help and use yellow balls as they turn black against the sun and are easier to see.

**4** Grip the club tighter when playing from soggy or wet ground - to avoid catching the ground before the ball and spoiling the shot - grip the club tighter. This reduces muscle movement and makes the swing slightly stiffer producing a clean strike from these difficult conditions. It may be necessary to take one club larger to produce the same power and distance.

**5** Keep warm on cold days - use hot pads - a sachet, which through a chemical reaction produces heat for approximately 6 hours. Consider wearing two gloves or gloves with Gore-Tex backing to protect your hands from cold wind. A great deal of body heat is lost through the head so wear a hat in cold weather.

# Practice & Preparation

**1** Forget everything you have been taught - when you're playing the game of golf the aim is to get the ball in the hole in the least number of shots possible. Many players suffer after a lesson because they try to make changes to their swing on the course. So, when you're playing the game forget the lesson and let the new ideas integrate themselves instinctively.

**2** Improve your swing on the driving range - the driving range is where you improve your swing and technique. The ball is only there to relieve the boredom. Don't worry where or how the ball is going - concentrate on the swing and the changes you're trying to make.

**3** Warm-up before you play - as in all sports it's essential to warm-up your muscles before you play. Unfortunately many golfers rush from the car park to the first tee only to see their ball slice out of bounds or dribble a few yards. Ideally you should arrive at least two hours before playing. Hit 100 balls on the driving range, practice chipping and putting and get to the tee with at least ten minutes to spare. Unfortunately this is not often possible for most amateur golfers. So, at the very least do some stretching exercises before you leave home, particularly stretching the back muscles.

**4** Practise 3-foot putts before you play - in previous practice putting sessions you will have attempted long putts and created muscle memory. Just before you play practise short putts. 3 foot or under. These are the putts that many golfers miss - particularly on the first few greens. Practising these short putts will build your confidence for the game ahead.

**5** Keep your equipment clean - the grooves in the clubface help give the ball spin so it's necessary to keep your clubs clean and in good condition. Never use new shoes for a full round of golf. Many golfers have had to retire from a round due to blisters made by new shoes. Wear comfortable clothing. Carry additional gloves and an umbrella in wet weather. Prepare all your equipment before playing.

# Fitness

**1** Exercise regularly - golf is a sport like any other sport and a player who is fit will have more chance of winning. If you are tired after 14 holes, the last four holes may be crucial to your chances of success. Walking is one of the best forms of building stamina. So if that buggy looks appealing... sometimes say no.

**2** Warm Up - one of the best exercise routines for golf is to take just five minutes before you play... lie flat on your back and pull your legs towards your chest. Slowly pull your legs closer to your chest as this will stretch your back and make you supple for the game. Only undertake this exercise if you feel you are able to do so without creating any injury.

**3** Eat the right food - top players usually eat fresh or dried fruit on the course to maintain a constant sugar level in their blood. Avoid eating heavy foods such as a full English breakfast before playing. Avoid eating chocolate on the course as this will give you a temporary rise in your blood sugar level but its effect will quickly fade. The wrong foods will cause tiredness and adversely affect your game and subsequent score.

**4** Drink water - sugary drinks have the same effect as chocolate. A temporary high then a fall in sugar levels creating a feeling of tiredness. Fizzy drinks can fill the body with gas, creating uncomfortable feelings and restricted movement. Water is the most beneficial liquid you can take whilst playing.

**5** Build your strength - each golfer has a stronger hand and a weaker hand. Undertake exercises to build the strength of your weaker hand... such as pulling the trolley or carrying the bag. Golf is a game played with both hands on the club and if you are strong with both hands it will improve your game.

# Budget

**1** Get value for money - calculate how many rounds you'll play with a set of clubs and divide that number into the cost of a new set of clubs. You'll find that new clubs are extremely good value for money and enable you to perform at the best of your ability. For example: If a new set of clubs costs £1000 and you play 50 rounds each year for 5 years - that's only £4 per round. Extremely good value for the better results you'll achieve.

**2** Spend money on a great putter - many golfers will spend a fortune on the driver, which they may only use, on average, 11 times in a round. However a putter may be used 30 to 40 times per round. Invest in a great putter taking advice from your professional. Remember the old expression: "drive for show... putt for dough!"

**3** Don't be fooled into thinking that golf is expensive - in years gone by golf was considered an elitist sport. Those days have gone and anyone of any age and any sex can now play golf. Golf can be fun and enjoyed by everybody.

**4** Consider joining a golf club - there are numerous benefits to joining a golf club. Social activities as well as golfing competitions. When you calculate the number of rounds you'll play - for your membership cost - you'll find it's great value for money. For example: If membership is £1000 and you play 80 rounds in a year - that's only £12.50 per round. And, of course, there are many other advantages and benefits. Golf competitions, social events and the opportunity to make new friends.

Key thoughts:

# Equipment

1. Have your clubs checked by a professional - all golfers are different. Have your clubs checked regularly by a professional to make certain that they suit your personal specifications. Areas that can make a huge difference are - grip size, shaft flex and the lie of the clubhead. Nobody would consider walking round a golf course in shoes that were one size too small... however many golfers use clubs that are not suited to them and wonder why they do not score as well as they might.

2. Carry the correct number of clubs - the maximum number of clubs you can carry is 14 and the minimum is 4. (With only 4 clubs one needs to be a putter) Often conditions indicate that is not always necessary to carry a full set. At times, using a half-set will help you learn to adapt and use different clubs for different situations.

3. Keep up-to-date - golf technology moves at a fast pace. The introduction of titanium and other materials has not only made the game easier but more enjoyable for many golfers. If your clubs are out of date consider changing them otherwise you will be at a disadvantage against other players using more up-to-date equipment.

4. Use the right ball - there are two main pieces of equipment used in a golf shot. One is the club the other is the ball. Many golfers will spend a great deal of money buying the right clubs and then use of the oldest, scruffiest ball in the bag. You will have greater distance and greater accuracy using a ball that suits you. Try different balls to find the one that's right for you. Make certain that your ball is always free from any debris or scuffs and grazes. Damage to the ball will drastically affect its aerodynamics and you may lose direction and distance. Ask your professional for advice on the correct ball for you. Professional players change the ball every few holes, some even every hole if damaged. The ball is an essential part of your equipment - treat it as such.

5. Look after your equipment - after a game played in wet conditions make certain that you dry your clubs in room temperature. Store them with the grips facing down to allow any water which has entered the club to run out.

6. Avoid putting tee pegs in the hole in the end of the grip - the hole in the end of the grip allows water to escape after a game played in the rain. A tee peg will prevent this happening and the water will damage your club. The only time to put a tee peg in the grips is when playing in the rain - to keep the grips off the bottom of the bag. (Remember to remove them!)

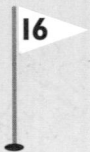

# Scoring & Games

**1** Handicaps - the handicap is a measurement of a golfer's ability against the course. It's the number of shots a player can use to better the par of the course. The system of handicap reduction is complicated. The basics of handicap are as follows. If a player completes a round in 90 shots with par for the course at 72 then that player's handicap would be 18. (90 - 72 = 18). A player reduces their handicap by reducing their shots over par. eg. If an 18-handicap player completes a par 72 course in 85 shots they are five under par. The player's handicap would be reduced by a percentage of the shots under par. Refer to your professional.

**2** Medal play - for higher handicap players this is one of the most difficult games to play, every shot counts. Two terms that are relevant are gross and nett. Gross is the total number of shots you have taken to play the 18 holes. Nett is the figure you are left with after deducting your handicap. eg. Gross score 90 less handicap of 20 = nett score 70.

**3** Stableford - a favourite amongst golfers. It's based on a points system per hole. It allows golfers who have one or more high-scoring holes to still have a chance of winning. Points are allocated, allowing for handicap, against each hole individually. Scoring is as follows. Bogey (1 over par) = 1 point. Par = 2 points. Birdie (1 under par) = 3 points. Eagle (2 under par) = 4 points. Albatross (3 under par) = 5 points. The beauty of the Stableford scoring system is that your round is not ruined by one bad hole.

**4** Matchplay - this game can be played with two or four players and it's a contest for each hole. With two players, allowing for handicap difference, the lower scoring player wins the whole. With two teams of two players the lower score of each side, allowing for handicap difference, wins the hole for that team. When a player or a team has won more holes than there are left to play they have won. eg. if the team is ahead by 4 holes with only 3 holes left to play they've won 4 and 3. A player/team is "dormie" when they are the same number of holes up - as there are holes left to play.

**5** Foursomes - this is a game played in pairs and is ideal for new golfers. The game is played with one ball per pair with the players in that team hitting alternate shots until each hole is completed. This is a tactical game where the strengths and weaknesses of each partner should be considered before driving off from the first tee. An ideal place to see foursomes in action is The Ryder Cup.

**6** Greensomes - this version of the game of golf is often used in mixed competitions because both players drive from each tee and then - decide which is the best drive. Subsequent shots are played alternately by each player - as in foursomes.

# Etiquette

**1** Dress appropriately - with modern fashion many golfers have become confused as to what is considered acceptable golfing attire. Avoid wearing studded pocket trousers - as this is the real definition of jeans. Jeans are not acceptable wear on golf courses. Shirts should have collars and be tucked into the trousers. Shoes must be golfing shoes not trainers or pumps. The correct shoes with studs will improve your grip when walking - a safety consideration. If you are considering wearing shorts - these should be of the tailored variety. Check with the golf club staff as to the length of socks to be worn with shorts at the course.

**2** Keep it going - one of the most frustrating situations for all golfers is - slow play! Keep up with the game ahead of you - don't be concerned about keeping ahead of the game behind you. If you find that you are falling behind the game in front and the game behind you plays quickly - do the sensible thing - and call them through. If the whole course is extremely busy then simply be patient and explain to the group behind that there's nowhere to go!

**3** Use the 3 R's - Replace your divots, rake the bunkers and repair your pitch marks!

**4** Ensure you're insured - in these days of increased litigation it's a great idea to have public liability insurance - just in case you hit someone with a ball (or club) and they sue you! It is unlikely that your household insurance will cover you in these situations.

**5** Be aware of other players - look around and ensure that your shout of joy at sinking a 60 foot putt isn't just at the time that another player is teeing off behind you. Golf is a game played in complete silence at the time of the shot.

**6** Avoiding walking on someone's line - on the green be careful to walk around the line of someone else's putt. This common courtesy is what sets golf apart from many other sports. Golfers do everything possible to make certain that they do not influence their opponent's play in any negative way. It's a game for sports men and women.

**7** Gamesmanship should be avoided at all costs - enough said!

# The **Rules**

Following is a short selection of common rules. This is not intended to be a definitive list or a full explanation of the exact rules. There is no substitute for the rule book.

**1** Get a book of rules - you can obtain a free book of rules from most golf clubs. Two great publications that are available are: Golf Rules Illustrated ISBN: 0600597075PB and Decisions on The Rules of Golf - ISBN 0600598470HB. (Published by Hamlyn Books). Read your rule book and be aware of the basics. It is unlikely that you will remember all the rules - so carry the rule book in your golf bag. Here is a short selection of rules that come into play on a regular basis for most golfers.

**2** Be aware of local rules - these are rules set by the golf club of the course you are playing. You will find them on the back of the score card. The rules are unique to each course - be certain to check them before playing. A classic example is - stones in bunkers! Some courses allow you to remove them - other courses don't!

**3** Lost Ball - Remember the ball is never deemed - lost! You just can't find it! This is a stroke and distance penalty - this means that you return to the point where the shot was played - add one penalty shot - and play the shot again. For example: You play a ball from the teeing ground into trees. You can't find it. You must return to the teeing ground again and play another ball. You will now have taken 3 shots. This is called "Three off the tee". A ball is also 'lost' if you cannot identify the ball as yours.

**4** Provisional Ball - if you believe that the ball you have played may be lost - you may play a provisional ball and continue playing it until you reach the place where you believe your original ball may be situated. You must declare to your playing partners/opponents that you are playing a provisional ball and be able to identify it as the provisional. For example: Put a mark on the ball or let the other players know the make and number and the fact that these details differ from the original ball.

**5** Out of Bounds - the out of bounds line is defined by white stakes and/or a white line. This is another stroke and distance penalty - return to the point from which you played the shot, add one shot to your score and play the shot again. NB: You must not remove the white stakes in any circumstances. For example - your ball has come to rest against a white stake and is still in bounds - you must play the shot as it lies or take a penalty drop.

**6** Unplayable Lie - you may declare the ball as unplayable at any place on the course - except in a water hazard. You have three choices: 1. Play another ball from the original point from which you played the shot. 2. Drop a ball within two club lengths of the unplayable ball (not nearer the hole) 3. Drop a ball behind the point where the unplayable ball lies - keeping that point directly between the hole and the place on which the ball is dropped. You may go back as far as you like. In all cases it is a penalty drop of one shot. When taking a drop, mark the current position of the ball (using a tee peg) without moving the ball. Next - using your longest club - measure out the point at which you can drop the ball - within the rules. Mark that position with a tee peg. Remove your club before dropping the ball. The ball is dropped from shoulder height at arm's length within the two marked points. Do not impart any spin to the ball when dropping it. If the ball, having been dropped, rolls closer to the hole than the original point - then you must re-drop.

7 Water Hazards Red and Yellow Stakes - Red stakes define the boundary of a lateral water hazard. When the ball enters this hazard make a note of the entry point. You have three choices. 1. Play a ball from the original position again. 2. Drop a ball behind the hazard - keeping the point of entry in a straight line between you and the flag. 3. You may drop a ball 2 club lengths to the side of the hazard at the point of entry. Yellow stakes define the boundary of a water hazard. You have two choices: . Play a ball from the original position again. 2. Drop a ball behind the hazard - keeping the point of entry in a straight line between you and the flag. In all cases it is a penalty drop of one shot.

8 Ground Under Repair - GUR and Staked Trees - this GUR area is defined by blue posts or a painted line accompanied by a sign or painted grass sign stating - GUR. You may take a free drop, within two club lengths, no nearer the hole from the nearest point of relief. For example: The nearest point of relief may be in the rough - you still have to drop there. You may be able to play from the area of GUR - unless prevented from doing so by local rules. Staked trees are young tress that have either a stake or banding (see local rules). The ball may be lifted and dropped without penalty - within two club lengths of the point where you can make a swing without touching the tree.

If you breech the rules in a stroke play game the penalty is 2 shots or disqualification. In match play - loss of the hole or disqualification.

The above explanations are by way of simple example - it is essential that you familiarise yourself with the exact rules in a recognised rule book.

Golf is a game, a game to be enjoyed. It's the ideal way to make new friends, get involved in social activities and travel to some of the most beautiful places on the planet. Use every golfing occasion to improve your game, to enjoy the scenery and to reach the goals you've set for yourself. With the advent of superior clubs and balls even advancing age won't stop you being able to still drive it far down the fairway, get backspin on the greens and shoot a score of which you're justly proud.

# Danny Peck

Danny has been playing golf for over 20 years. He bring a special insight to the game by his studies of Psychology, Sports Therapy and Golfing Technique. His time as a teaching professional has enabled him to appreciate the fact that simple techniques are the fundamentals of success.

As a PGA qualified professional Danny has played and won a number of tournaments in the UK. Danny was nominated for Professional of the Year in 2000 in the prestigious Clubhaus Awards.

As an attendee on three separate occasions at the World Teaching Seminar he has studied with and gained insights from some of the best teachers in the world of golf today such as - David Leadbetter - Butch Harman - Dr. Robert Rotella.

The success of his students is ample evidence that his approach to teaching the game of golf - really works.

As Head Of Golf Operations at the renowned Warwickshire Golf Club Danny is in charge of a professional coaching team giving instructions to golfers of all ages and abilities. The most regular feedback from his pupils is that "Danny makes it so simple to understand and so simple to put into practice!"

# Peter Thomson

Peter Thomson is now regarded as the UK's leading strategist on personal and business growth. Starting in business in 1972 he built 3 successful companies - selling the last to a public company, after only 5 years trading, enabling him to retire at age 42.

Since that time Peter has concentrated on sharing his proven methods for business and personal success via audio and video programmes, books, seminars and conference speeches.

With over 60 audio programmes, 30 video programmes recorded and 3 books written he is Nightingale Conant's leading UK author.

Peter is the publisher, writer and presenter of the widely acclaimed personal development AUDIO newsletter "THE ACHIEVER'S EDGE!" And - SALES AT THE EDGE - a monthly Video/CD/cassette - sales meeting system - for busy sales managers, sales directors and business owners.

In 1999 The American Intercontinental University in London - with permission granted by the American Government- awarded Peter an Honorary Doctorate (Doctor of Letters) for his work in communication skills and helping others to succeed in life.

As a family man and keen golfer he has seen his handicap consistently reduce by application of the ideas in this book.

# How to **promote** your **business** with booklets

1. As a gift to prospective customers
2. As a bonus for re-joining as a member (Golf Club, Tennis Club, Magazine)
3. Give Tips Booklet to people or organisations who can refer business to you
4. As a bonus for responding to an advert or direct mail offering
5. Send a Tips Booklet to your customers at year's end - thanking them for their business
6. Use a Tips Booklet as a thank you for a sales appointment
7. Mail a Tips Booklet to your prospect list to stay in touch with them
8. Use it as a Christmas card - the cover can be overprinted
9. Offer a Tips Booklet as a bonus if someone replies to a time-sensitive offer
10. Offer a Tips Booklet as a bonus for a sale of a certain size
11. Give the booklet away at a trade fair or exhibition to attract more potential customers to your stand
12. Give a Tips Booklet as an incentive for completing a Customer Survey Form
13. Include a Tips Booklet as a "Thank You" for the order, when sending an invoice or statement
14. Bundle or package a Tips Booklet as a value added bonus for ordering a particular product from your range
15. Send an appropriate Tips Booklet to your staff as a reminder of some of the key principles of success - or as a thank you for a job well done
16. Use packs of Tips Booklets as prizes in a raffle or charity appeal
17. Give a Tips Booklet to the first 50 people who come to your shop or business
18. As a bonus for sponsorship activation
19. Use a Tips Booklet to launch a new product - including product details in the centre pages of the booklet
20. Use a Tips Booklet as a memorable Change of Address card

# Booklet Request

**Yes**, please send me _____ copies of "Golf 97 Surprisingly Simple Secrets - How you can turn Frustration into Pleasure" at only £6.97 + 30p Postage & Packing each.

## Overprinting

☐ Please let me have details on how to personalise the booklets with my company logo and details. (Please tick)

## Other Booklets

☐ Please let me have details of the other tip booklets in the series. (Please tick)

## Your Details

| | |
|---|---|
| Mr/Mrs/Ms: | |
| Company: | |
| Position: | |
| Address: | |
| | Post Code: |
| Telephone: | |
| Email: | Date: |

## Payment Details

**I enclose my cheque for £_____** (payable to Peter Thomson International Plc)

**Please debit my** Access ☐    Visa ☐    MasterCard ☐   **For £_____**

**Card Number**: ☐☐☐☐ ☐☐☐☐ ☐☐☐☐ ☐☐☐☐

**Expiry Date**: ☐☐ ☐☐

*Peter Thomson International Plc may occasionally offer your name and address details to other reputable companies who wish to contact you with information. If you do not wish to receive these offers, please tick the box* ☐

## Signature:

## Card Holder Name:

Peter Thomson International Plc
PO Box 666 Royal Leamington Spa Warwickshire United Kingdom CV32 6YP
Tel: +44 (0) 1926 339901  Fax: +44 (0) 1926 339139
Email: action@peterthomson.com  Website: www.peterthomson.com

**If you are interested in retailing these booklets please tick this box** ☐